Discovering

BUGS

George McGavin

Illustrations by Wendy Meadway

The Bookwright Press
New York · 1989

Discovering Nature

First published in the
United States in 1989 by
The Bookwright Press
387 Park Avenue South
New York, NY 10016

First published in 1988 by
Wayland (Publishers) Limited
61 Western Road, Hove
East Sussex BN3 1JD, England

© Copyright 1988 Wayland (Publishers) Limited

Typeset by DP Press Ltd., Sevenoaks, Kent
Printed in Italy by Sagdos S.p.A., Milan

Cover *A group of harlequin-bug nymphs cluster together on a leaf for protection.*

Frontispiece *The tropical lantern bug has a strange, bulbous head with markings on it that make it look like a fierce animal.*

Library of Congress Cataloging-in-Publication Data

McGavin, George.
  [Discovering bugs]
  Bugs / by George McGavin.
    p.   cm.—(Discovering nature)
  First published in 1988 in England under title: Discovering bugs.
  Bibliography: p.
  Includes index.
  Summary: Describes the physical characteristics, life cycles, defenses, types, and behavior of bugs.
    ISBN 0–531–18226–6
  1. Insects—Juvenile literature. [1. Insects.] I. Title. II. Series.
QL467.2.M37 1989
595.7—dc19

88–19406
CIP
AC

Contents

1
Introducing Bugs

A long-legged water measurer feeds on a water flea. The bug pierces the flea's body with its long rostrum.

What Is a Bug?

Most people use the word bug to mean any insect or "creepy-crawly." In fact, the word should be used only when talking about a very particular group of insects. These insects are the *Hemiptera*. The name comes from the Greek words meaning half (*hemi*) and wing (*pteron*).

There are over one million known kinds of insects, and of these, 67,500 are bugs. They have been around for over 300 million years, and in this time they have developed many strange shapes and habits. Like other insects, bugs have three pairs of legs, three divisions of the body (the head, **thorax** and **abdomen**) and usually, two pairs of wings. They differ from other insects in the way they eat. Bugs have mouthparts, called the **rostrum**, shaped like a long, pointed beak, through which they suck their food.

You might mistake some kinds of bug for beetles, but if you look closely and see a beak instead of jaws you will know it is a sucking bug, rather than a chewing beetle.

Most bugs are **herbivores** and many are serious pests because they destroy crops. Others are helpful to humans because they eat insects.

Bugs are mostly active insects with well-developed **compound eyes**. They can sing, jump and swim. They range in size from the tiny whiteflies to the giant water bugs.

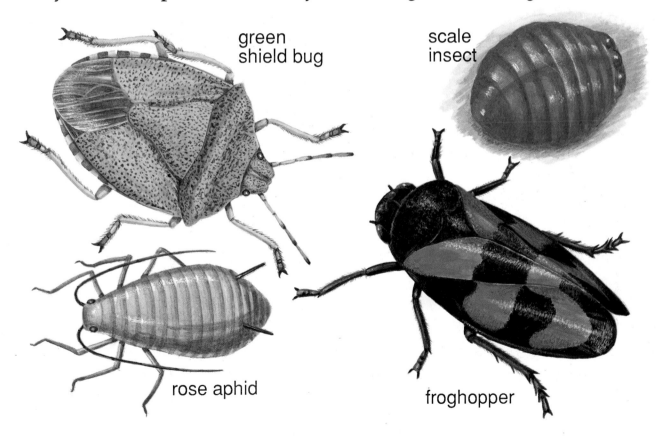

green shield bug

scale insect

rose aphid

froghopper

The Bug's Body

Bugs are divided into two quite different groups, the *Heteroptera* and the *Homoptera*. The main difference between them is in their front wings. The name *Heteroptera* comes from two Greek words, *heteros*, meaning different, and *pteron*, meaning a wing. These bugs are sometimes called the true bugs. Their front wings are divided into two areas — tough at the base and soft at the tip. This group includes colorful shield bugs, beautifully ornamented lace bugs, long-legged stilt bugs, fierce assassin bugs, bloodthirsty bedbugs, squash bugs, flat bugs, backswimmers, water boatmen and water scorpions.

The *Homoptera* get their name from the Greek words *homos*, meaning the same, and *pteron*. That is because the front wings are an even texture all over. The *Homoptera* do

Brightly colored shield bugs feed on a seed head. They are heteropteran bugs, with their wings folded flat over their bodies.

not have a collective common name, but the group includes aphids, planthoppers, cicadas, scale insects, whiteflies, spittle bugs and lantern bugs. Together these two groups are called the *Hemiptera*, or bugs.

Heteroptera hold their wings flat over their backs when resting, but the *Homoptera* hold their wings like a house roof over their backs. The head carries the sucking mouthparts, a pair of compound eyes (except in some cases such as the **parasitic** batbugs, which do not have eyes) and a pair of **antennae** made up of several segments. The thorax is the powerhouse of the insect and carries two pairs of wings and three pairs of legs. The abdomen contains the digestive and reproductive systems.

A cicada from Sarawak rests on a leaf. Its wings are raised over its back, which shows that it is a homopteran bug.

Shapes and Sizes

Bugs can be found in all shapes and sizes, from the tiny, elegant whiteflies, and scale insects, which look like warts on the surface of plants, to large broad-bodied water bugs. The back of the thorax of some treehoppers is enlarged into fantastic shapes. Some bugs look like ants or beetles, while others have wings that look like intricate lacework. Legs can be very long and slender for walking on water, or short and strong for grasping food. Many shield bugs and squash bugs are strangely shaped, with spiny or flattened projections on the legs, thorax or other parts of the body.

It would be impossible to describe fully even a tiny number of the thousands of wonderful shapes and bizarre forms that can be found in the bug world, but lantern bugs should have a special mention. Lantern bugs

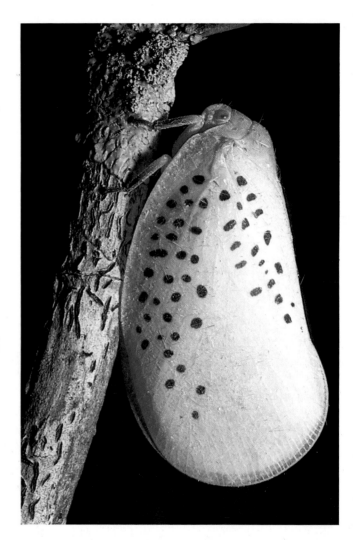

This tropical homopteran bug has very large wings, which cover its body when folded.

can be up to 8 cm (3 in) long and are found in the tropical regions of the world. They can be brightly colored or **camouflaged**, but all have a strange, **bulbous** head, which looks out of proportion to the rest of the

This delicate thread-legged bug from Trinidad feeds on gnats and midges.

body. One kind of lantern bug found in Brazil has head markings that make it look like a crocodile. The lantern bug originally got its name because people thought that the strange head glowed in the dark.

However peculiar we think a bug may look, there is probably a very good reason for its appearance.

2

Bugs Everywhere

A water scorpion takes in air from the surface of the water through its snorkel.

Bugs and Water

All bugs found living on or in water are *Heteroptera*. Around almost any pond, stream, lake or river you will find bugs. There are even some bugs, called oceanstriders, that live at sea.

Bugs like pondskaters and waterstriders can walk on the surface of water because they are small, they have special water-repelling feet, and the surface of the water acts like an elastic sheet, which is difficult for them to break through.

There are almost 1,500 kinds of bugs that live on the water's surface, and they are all **predators**. The surface of water provides a constant supply of fresh food in the form of small insects that fall onto it. Struggling insects soon attract the water-walking bugs, which have hairs on their legs that sense vibration and large eyes to detect prey. The helpless

The oceanstrider spends all its time at sea.

A long-legged pondskater strides across the water's surface in pursuit of its prey.

victims, trapped by the water's surface, are pierced and sucked dry.

Below the surface there are well over 1,000 other kinds of bugs, such as water boatmen, backswimmers and water scorpions. Many of these bugs are predators like the surface bugs, but others sieve fine particles of food from the water, using their hairy front legs.

Underwater, bugs breathe either by taking down thin films of air trapped by their velvety body hairs, or by having a long breathing tube or snorkel at the end of the abdomen which they stick up through the surface of the water. The water scorpion got its name because its snorkel makes it look like a scorpion.

Water scorpions and giant water bugs have large grasping front legs and can catch and kill quite large food items, such as tadpoles and small fish.

Bugs on Land

The vast majority of all bugs are found on land. They live in all sorts of places — on or under bark, under stones or leaf litter, in rotting logs, on flowers, leaves and every other part of all kinds of plants and trees. Some bugs live on the shore, or on floating mats of vegetation, in piles of stored grain, on fresh animal dung and even in the nests of birds and bats. No matter where you are in the world you can find interesting bugs if you take the time to look carefully. That tiny blob on a plant is probably a scale insect; moving **lichen** may well be a camouflaged shield bug; and those sharp thorns could be disguised treehoppers.

Some kinds of bugs are very common and have become pests that destroy crops, while others are so rare that nothing is known about the way

A group of shiny black heteropteran bugs like these can be mistaken for beetles.

they live. There must be many hundreds of unknown kinds of bugs still waiting to be discovered.

Like most insects living on land, they breathe by taking air in through a series of small holes along the sides of their bodies. The air fills a complicated system of tubes inside the bug's body, and is eventually absorbed.

Most land-living bugs are herbivores that suck the juices of plants in various ways. The rest are carnivores, which feed on the contents of insects' bodies, or bloodsuckers, which suck the blood of various mammals, including humans.

These leaf-footed bug nymphs give off an unpleasant smell if disturbed.

Cinch bugs gather in a hollow plant stalk for protection during winter.

3

A Bug's Life Cycle

Two leaf-footed bugs mating. The female may go off to feed, taking the male too.

Courtship and Mating

Like all other animals, bugs have to reproduce themselves to leave behind offspring of their own kind before they die. The first step is to find the right mate. Courtship is a way of attracting a mate, and can be done using sight, smell or sound. Each type of bug can recognize its own kind and this makes sure that no time or energy is wasted making mistakes.

Bugs often attract a mate with mating calls. Many kinds of bugs can make sounds by rubbing two parts of the body together. Shield bugs and bark bugs rub parts of their legs across their abdomens, for example.

Some female bugs attract the males with a song, and then the males respond by singing the correct courtship song. The most famous singers in the bug world are the cicadas. Male cicadas have a pair of

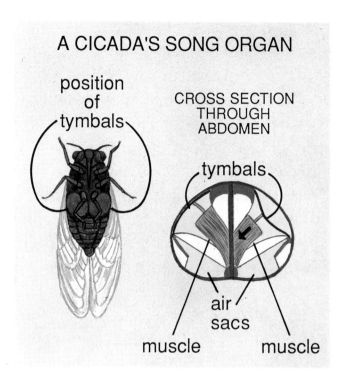

A CICADA'S SONG ORGAN

position of tymbals

CROSS SECTION THROUGH ABDOMEN

tymbals

air sacs

muscle

muscle

has its own song so that the right female will be attracted.

Once male and female bugs have found each other, mating can begin and, for some bugs, it can last for hours. The female then produces fertile eggs. Needless to say, however, there are exceptions to any rule. For instance, some aphids reproduce without involving males at all. They do not produce eggs but give birth to live young.

An aphid giving birth to fully formed young rather than eggs.

special sound-producing organs called **tymbals** at the base of the abdomen. The tymbal is like a drumskin covering a hollow chamber. Muscles attached to the undersides of the tymbals make them click in and out at high speed. Cicada calls can be heard from far away, and each kind of cicada

Eggs

Bugs' eggs do not all look the same. They can be small and rounded, they may have stalks, or beautiful surface patterns. Female bugs usually lay their eggs through an **ovipositor**, singly or in groups, on or in plant tissues, soil and leaf litter. Some giant water bugs lay their eggs on the back of the male.

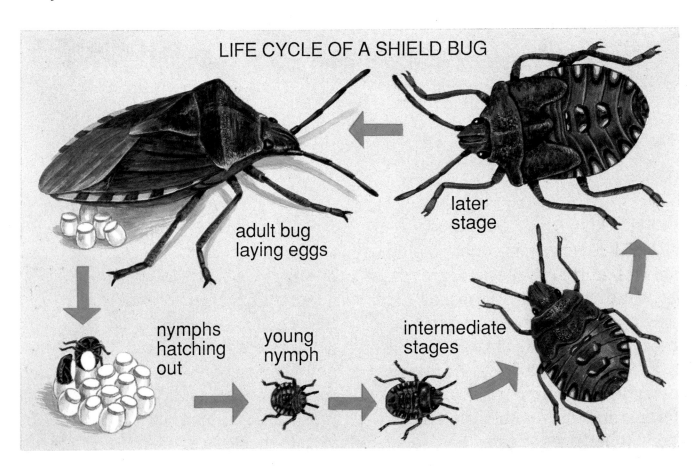

LIFE CYCLE OF A SHIELD BUG

adult bug laying eggs

later stage

nymphs hatching out

young nymph

intermediate stages

A water bug carries his partner's eggs.

Eggs can make tasty meals for predators, so some bugs guard their eggs. The female parent bug, a kind of shield bug, will stand guard over her eggs and, even after they hatch, the young bugs get some protection because the female stays with them until they are quite large. Young bugs, or **nymphs**, will even follow the female and shelter underneath her body when danger threatens.

The eggs are also in danger of drying out. So protection is provided when the eggs are laid inside plant tissues.

Many eggs have a removable lid to help the young nymphs escape when they are ready to hatch. Some nymphs have a detachable spine on their heads to help them break open the eggshell.

Young Bugs

The young stages in the life cycle of insects like butterflies and flies do not look much like the adults they eventually become. In contrast, bugs,

A harlequin bug sheds its old skin and reveals a soft new covering. It is very vulnerable until the new skin hardens.

and some other insect groups, produce nymphs that look very

much like the adults and usually feed on the same things. Nymphs differ from adults in that they do not have wings and cannot reproduce.

When the young nymphs hatch from their eggs, they begin to feed and grow. The time a bug spends as a nymph varies enormously, from a few weeks to the incredible 17-year development of some kinds of cicada nymph. They live underground and feed on a very poor diet of watery root juices.

Like all insects, bugs have their skeletons on the outside, in the form of tough waterproof skin called the exoskeleton (exo is a Greek word meaning outside). Every so often, the old skin becomes too small for the growing nymphs, so they shed it, or molt, to reveal a new, soft skin underneath. The new skin soon hardens. Most heteropteran bugs shed their skin five times; and homopteran bugs molt between three and seven times before they become fully formed adults. The nymphs grow their wings on the outside and each time they molt you can see the wing buds getting bigger.

Nymphs have special glands in their abdomens which make bad-smelling chemicals. These chemicals are used to ward off predators.

The strange form of this treehopper nymph mimics the tendrils it is sitting on.

4

Bug Lifestyles

Using its strong front legs to hold its prey, this shield bug sucks out the body of a beetle grub.

The Perfect Suckers

Heteropteran bugs can swing their mouthparts forward when they feed. This is very useful for **carnivorous** bugs when they attack large items of prey because it means that they can feed without having to climb on top of their meal. The rostrum through which bugs suck their liquid food is very efficient.

The mouthparts have two pairs of long filaments called **stylets**. These stylets fit closely together in a bundle and are joined by lengthwise ridges and grooves. The stylets are enclosed by an outer covering called the **labium**. The labium is usually made up of several segments so that it can fold back when the stylets are being pushed into food. The tip of the labium has special sense organs that tell the bug if the food is edible or not.

The outer pair of stylets, called

mandibles, have sharp points and teeth that face backward, making it easy for the bug to saw its mouthparts into food. The inner pair of stylets, called maxillae, have two hollow channels for saliva to pass down and for the liquid food to be sucked up. Bugs need saliva to predigest semi-solid food so that it can pass up the narrow food channel.

Mouthparts are not identical in all species because bugs eat different foods. The assassin bugs, for example, have short and curved mouthparts for stabbing through insects' bodies. In contrast, the flat bugs have very long mouthparts for probing under bark in search of food.

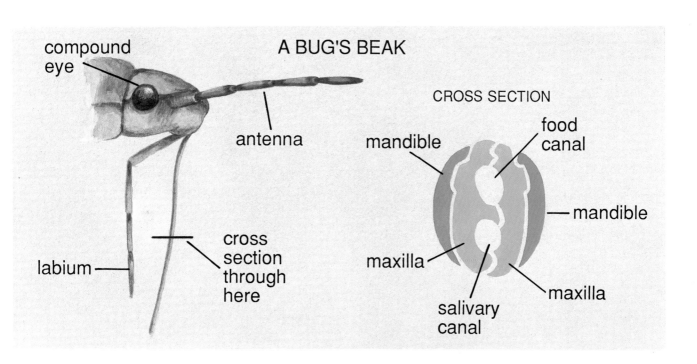

A BUG'S BEAK

compound eye

antenna

labium

cross section through here

CROSS SECTION

mandible

food canal

mandible

maxilla

salivary canal

maxilla

Hunters and Plant-eaters

There is a great difference between being a carnivore and being a herbivore. Carnivorous bugs such as backswimmers, assassin bugs, waterstriders and flower bugs may have difficulty holding onto their meal if it is a large, active insect. There are several answers to this problem. One is to have spiny, grasping front legs; another is to inject a swift-acting, paralyzing saliva into the victim.

Some bugs even lie in wait and ambush their prey. Others have barbs on their mouthparts so that they can anchor their meals firmly while they suck out the body contents. Many kinds of carnivorous bugs attack slow-moving insects, such as caterpillars, and do not need to use any special

A water scorpion feeds on a young stickleback it has just caught.

hunting methods.

Although plants do not run away, a bug still has to hold on to feed. Many plants have spines or waxy surfaces to discourage bugs; and some plants have special tiny hairs with sticky capsules at their tips which are designed to break when bugs brush against them. The bugs try to clean their legs and mouthparts and just end up becoming more and more entangled.

Some plant-eating bugs, such as aphids and scale insects, do not have to move a great deal. Once they have found a good place to feed they simply insert their mouthparts into the plant and hold on.

One problem with feeding on plants is that the food is not always very nutritious. Bugs can deal with poor food by eating large amounts of it, or by developing at a slower rate. Many herbivorous bugs eat **dilute**

These leaf-footed nymphs from Costa Rica are feeding on vine tendrils.

food, so large amounts of waste are produced by the digestive system. Some planthoppers can shoot their waste products well away from where they are feeding, and some even aim them at their enemies.

Unusual Bugs

Carnivorous bugs can be very clever at catching their food. Ambush bugs, for example, can catch very large insects with their pincerlike front legs, armed with sharp spines. There are certain assassin bugs that stick soil, bits of dead plants and other rubbish onto their backs to disguise themselves as they approach their victims. Another ingenious bug, a species of assassin bug, smears sticky plant resin on its front legs and uses them to catch small insects.

This unusual assassin bug, which mimics a tarantula wasp, has caught a scarab beetle.

Ants can be fierce opponents, but there are amazing bugs that have special hairs that ooze a sweet but deadly fluid, attractive to ants. When the ants lick the hairs they are soon overpowered, and then the bug can suck them dry in safety.

There are also a few bugs that feed on insects that have become trapped by carnivorous plants. The bugs do not become trapped on the plant's sticky hairs because they walk very carefully and do not clean their feet.

Stilt bugs are slender, with incredibly long legs, and look a bit like animated pieces of thread. They feed on plants and sometimes on slow-moving insects such as aphids. Blood-sucking bedbugs can be found in houses, living around the baseboards and under floors. The nymphs and adults feed at night and leave their victims with an itchy red mark on their skin.

Covered with dust, bits of dead vegetation and earth, this assassin bug is barely visible as it stalks its prey.

Female bedbugs can suck up twice their own weight in blood at one meal, so it is not surprising that they can survive a whole year without any more food. Some peculiar bugs that feed only on bats' blood are wingless but have large claws for holding on to their furry hosts.

5

Bugs and Their Defenses

The black areas on the abdomen of this shield-bug nymph mark the three pairs of stink-gland openings.

Colors and Smells

Bugs must be able to defend themselves from being attacked and eaten by many other kinds of animals. Many *Homoptera*, such as froghoppers and planthoppers, jump very powerfully at the slightest hint of danger. Other bugs taste bad or smell horrible.

It would be of no use to a bug if predators found out that the bug was inedible only after attacking, so bugs advertise their horrible taste by being brightly colored. Predators soon learn to leave bright bugs alone. Black and red or orange are common warning colors in the insect world. Sometimes bugs can be quite good to eat but fool their enemies by looking the same as foul-tasting bugs.

Many kinds of heteropteran bugs are called stinkbugs. The name refers to the fact that the bugs have special

scent glands in the thorax that produce disgusting-smelling fluids. Special areas on the surface of the body trap the fluids so that the smell lingers longer. Some bugs squirt these fluids quite accurately at their attackers, while others smear the fluid onto their enemies. The defensive fluids may kill the predators if enough is absorbed through the skin, but usually the effect is temporary

The brilliant coloring of this shield bug from Sarawak protects it from its enemies.

irritation or blindness. While the predators recover from the shock, the bugs can make good their escape.

Nymphs are especially good targets for predators because they cannot fly away. So, for greater protection, they are often more brightly colored than the adults.

Camouflage

If a bug does not smell terrible and is not brightly colored it can defend itself by being difficult to see. Many bugs are colored to blend in perfectly with their background.

The eggs, nymphs and adults of some kinds of shield bug are camouflaged to look like lichen-covered bark, for example.

Camouflage is particularly

Cleverly disguised as a leaf, this plant-hopper avoids predators.

important for cicadas, which sing very noisily. You can always hear them but never see them because they match the tree trunks on which they sit. So, although camouflage can be just a simple color match of the background, you will often find bugs that are stippled or mottled as well, so that the outline of the body is difficult to see. Camouflage can also involve shape. For example, some leaf-footed bugs have flattened areas of the legs and antennae that make them look less like insects.

Camouflage is not always used as a defense. It also enables carnivorous bugs to catch their food. Ambush bugs can be well concealed in flowers, and assassin bugs carry their own home-made camouflage. It is much easier to camouflage yourself if you are very small and do not move around much.

Camouflage is particularly important for herbivorous bugs that

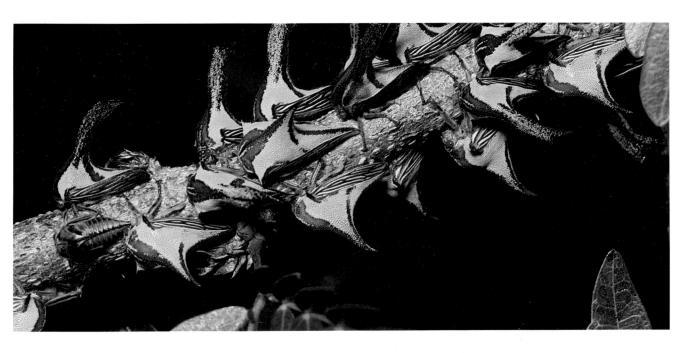

Above *A group of rain forest treehoppers look like thorns on a twig – all facing the same way to be most convincing.*

Right *To protect itself from predators, this leafhopper merges with the lichen it sits on.*

may feed for a long time in one place. Perhaps there are many kinds of bugs that have not yet been discovered because they are so well hidden.

Spines and Other Armor

A prickly pair of spiny South African bugs.

One way for a bug to defend itself is to be difficult to eat. Predators have so much trouble trying to eat it that they give up and look for an easier meal. There are many bugs that have spines and fairly tough skin.

The surface of the skin may also be covered with warts or lumps.

Armor need not always be hard. Many homopteran bugs produce all kinds of protective waxes in the form of threads, powders or sheets. Scale insects live inside a tough, waxy cover, which they build up as they grow. Others live inside masses of cottony wax, which makes them difficult for predators to eat.

The nymphs of spittle bugs and froghoppers live inside foam for protection. They make the foam by blowing air through their waste products, mixed with liquids from special glands at the end of the abdomen. The liquid waxy soap produced protects the nymphs from enemy attack.

Humans have made use of some of these defensive secretions. Scale insect waxes and resins have been used in the food and cosmetic industries. There is a bug's resin that is used to make a good-quality varnish called shellac. In Southeast Asia, planthopper wax has been used to make candles. A red dye, called cochineal, is extracted from the bodies

The gall louse produces lots of fine waxy threads to hide it from its enemies.

The resinous coating produced by scale insects is used to manufacture varnish.

of scale insects native to Mexico and Central America. They feed on cactus and approximately 70,000 bodies are needed to make 50 g (1¾ oz) of dye.

Wearing a Disguise

Bugs can be great impersonators. They can look like plants or other insects to avoid being attacked. Many kinds of heteropteran bug, such as plant bugs and seed bugs, imitate ants and wasps, which are usually fierce.

Bugs **mimic** other insects by having the same coloring or shape or by behaving in the same way. Sometimes all three methods are used, so predators that have learned to avoid the real thing will also avoid the bugs that are pretending.

Some bugs imitate foul-tasting beetles. Treehoppers are well known for their fantastic imitations of plant thorns or chewed leaves. The thorax of many treehoppers is extended into amazing designs, which vary from simple thorn shapes to bizarre and complex structures that look like ants. Sometimes these weird extensions seem bigger than the rest of the bug's body. Thorn-impersonating bugs feed in groups and point the same way

The fantastic shape of this treehopper's thorax disguises it as an ant. Its abdomen and wings merge into the color of the leaf it sits on.

to make their deception more convincing.

Scale insects do not look like insects at all. Many of them look like tiny warts or bumps that you might expect to find on a plant. Bugs who live in ant colonies tend to look like ants but there must be something

This treehopper from Trinidad is camouflaged as a dying leaf.

more that protects them from being eaten by their unwilling hosts. It is possible that the bugs make their disguise more perfect by moving and smelling like the ants.

6
Bugs and Their Enemies

A young lacewing feeding on aphids, using its sickle-shaped jaws. To protect themselves the aphids produce a liquid that sticks the larva's jaws together.

Despite the many ways in which bugs can protect themselves, there are predators who have found out how to beat their defenses. A bug's enemies include birds, reptiles, mammals, spiders, scorpions and many kinds of insects, including other bugs. Young flowerflies, young and adult lacewings and ladybugs are the most important enemies from the insect world. There are also many kinds of parasitic wasps that lay their eggs in the eggs or nymphs of bugs. Some kinds of large wasps and assassin bugs have learned to pull spittle-bug nymphs out of their protective froth.

Some bug enemies can be very useful to the farmer or gardener. A ladybug will eat up to 100 aphids each day, and a full-grown flowerfly grub can easily wipe out a whole aphid colony on its own. Lacewing grubs have a pair of hollow sickle-shaped jaws that they use to impale and

suck the aphids. The aphids strike back by making a sticky substance that sets solid in the hollow jaws. Lacewing grubs are often just as sneaky because they can disguise themselves by sticking the skins of previously eaten aphids onto their backs.

Aphids are not as defenseless as they may seem. Many kinds of aphids have a special relationship with ants that feed on their sweet waste products, called honeydew. In return for the honeydew, the ants protect the aphids from attack and even carry them to good feeding sites. It has been said that the ants farm the aphids like humans farm cows. Some ants even build shelters over the aphid colony.

Top *The body of an aphid becomes swollen and hard once a parasitic wasp has laid its egg inside.*
Left *Ladybug larvae preying on aphids.*

7

Bugs as Pests

This underground root aphid is attacking the roots of a head of lettuce.

Anyone who has a garden will know the damage that aphids and other bugs can do. In fact, there are few crops that escape bug attack. Bugs can weaken the plants by feeding on their tissues, or by infecting them with **viruses**, **bacteria** and **fungi**. The list of crops affected is very long and includes cotton, wheat, coffee, tea, potatoes, beets, soft fruits, millet, rice, vines and many vegetables.

The results of bug attack can be very serious. The European wine industry was nearly destroyed by a bug that was accidentally introduced and fed on the vines' roots. Sugarcane production in some parts of the world has been threatened by a kind of planthopper. Fortunately, scientists found another kind of bug that ate the eggs of the pest bug. Control of pests by biological means is called **biological control** and can be a better method than using expensive

Blood-sucking bugs, like this assassin bug, can transmit diseases.

the fact that it likes to bite its victims on the face and mouth.

But bugs are not all bad. Tiny scale insects have been used in Australia to control terrible weeds such as prickly pear. In Southeast Asia, masses of giant water bug eggs are eaten like caviar. The manna of Bible stories may well have been lumps of dried honeydew from scale insects.

chemical insecticides, which harm the environment. A very serious pest bug at the moment is the Asian rice brown planthopper.

Humans and animals can be bitten by blood-sucking bugs, some of which carry diseases. In North America, there is an assassin bug, about 1.7 cm (.7 in) long, which is called the kissing bug. It gets this charming name from

Tiny whiteflies are a terrible pest for greenhouse crops. They can be biologically controlled by introducing a small wasp that attacks them.

8
Learning More About Bugs

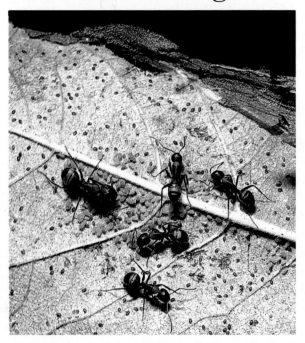

You will often see ants tending a colony of aphids in gardens.

The best way to learn about bugs is to study them at first hand. Almost any natural area, woodland, garden, pond or stream will contain enough bugs to keep you going for a long time. You may need some equipment but it can all be homemade.

A sweep net is good for collecting bugs from low-growing plants, and a sheet or tray can be used to catch bugs that you shake or beat from the branches of shrubs and trees. A magnifying glass is essential, and you need a notebook and pencil to record your field notes. A long-handled pond net and a large jam jar will enable you to catch and study most of the interesting water bugs.

Watch colonies of aphids. Are they being looked after by ants? Can you see any ladybugs eating the aphids? Count how many are eaten. If you are lucky you might even see a minute parasitic wasp laying her egg inside an

magnifying
glass

notebook
and
pencil

white
tray

A magnifying glass and a notebook and pencil are essential pieces of equipment for studying and recording what you find. Collect the bugs on a tray when you strike the branch and shake them off the leaves.

aphid's body. Then you could watch and see what happens as the wasp's grub develops inside.

Compare the numbers and kinds of bugs you find in different areas. Can you think of any reasons for the differences you find? If you keep bugs in a cage or glass tank, make sure that they have the right kind of food. Plant-eating bugs should be given a fresh supply of the food you found them on, or better still, a potted plant of the correct kind. Carnivorous bugs are not so fussy, and perhaps a colony of aphids placed in the cage will do the trick.

Use your magnifying glass and you will see that the small world of bugs is more fantastic than any science fiction story. We can always learn something new and useful from nature, and even when we think we know all about bugs, there are still many more surprises in store.

Glossary

Abdomen The rear part of an insect's body, joined to the thorax.

Antennae A pair of feelers on an insect's head that are sensitive to touch and smell.

Bacteria Microscopic organisms that exist everywhere, including the human body.

Biological control A method of controlling one kind of animal or plant by using another to attack it.

Bulbous Bulb-shaped.

Camouflaged Hidden by colorings and markings that blend in with the surroundings.

Carnivore An animal, or sometimes a plant, that eats animals.

Compound eyes Eyes made up of lots of different "seeing" units grouped together, so that the bug sees a lot of separate images, like a mosaic.

Dilute Watery.

Fungus (plural fungi) A plant without green coloring, such as mushrooms.

Herbivore An animal or insect that only eats plants.

Labium The lower lip of an insect. In bugs it forms a covering around the stylets.

Lichen A tiny fungus-like plant that grows on rocks and tree trunks.

Mimic To imitate the behavior or appearance of another animal so as to be protected from enemies.

Nymph The young stages of a developing insect, when it looks like the adult insect.

Ovipositor The egg-laying device in female insects.

Parasite An animal or plant that lives and feeds in or on another.

Predator An animal that kills and eats other animals.

Rostrum The long, beak-like extension of a bug's mouthparts; see stylets.

Stylets The long, pointed filaments that make up the bug's special piercing and sucking mouthparts.

Thorax The middle section of an insect's body that carries the wings and legs.

Tymbals Special sound-producing organs in cicadas.

Virus A minute organism, smaller than any bacterium, that causes disease.

Finding Out More

Donald J. Borror and Richard E. White, *A Field Guide to the Insects of America North of Mexico.* (Petersen Field Guide Series) Houghton Mifflin, 1974.

John Burton, *The Oxford Book of Insects.* Oxford University Press, 1981.

M. Chinery, *A Field Guide to the Insects of Britain and Northern Europe.* Greene-Viking Penguin, 1976.

Casey Horton, *Insects.* Gloucester Press, 1984.

Joyce Pope, *Insects.* Franklin Watts, 1985.

Picture Acknowledgments

All photographs are from Oxford Scientific Films by the following photographers: Kathie Atkinson cover, 22; G.I. Bernard 15 (right), 17 (left), 32, 33 (bottom), 39 (top); Waina Cheng 16; N.M. Collins 31; J.A.L. Cooke 12, 13, 21, 29, 35, 37, 39 (bottom), 40, 41; Stephen Dalton 23; P.J. De Vries 24, 28; Michael Fogden frontispiece, 27, 33 (top), 34, 36; Rodger Jackman 14; Breck P. Kent 28; Alastair Macewen 8; Colin Milkins 19, 26; Peter Parks 15 (left); K. Porter 17 (right); Alastair Shay 11, 18; David Thompson 42; Nick Woods 10, 30.

Index